A+
books

A Day in the Life of a
BALD EAGLE
A 4D BOOK

by Lisa J. Amstutz

Consultant: Robert T. Mason
Professor of Integrative Biology
J.C. Braly Curator of Vertebrates
Oregon State University

PEBBLE
a capstone imprint

Download the Capstone 4D app!

- Ask an adult to download the Capstone 4D app.
- Scan the cover and stars inside the book for additional content.

When you scan a spread, you'll find
fun extra stuff to go with this book!
You can also find these things
on the web at www.capstone4D.com
using the password: eagle.15183

A+ Books are published by Pebble
1710 Roe Crest Drive, North Mankato, Minnesota 56003
www.mycapstone.com

Library of Congress Cataloging-in-Publication Data
Names: Amstutz, Lisa J., author.
Title: A day in the life of a bald eagle : a 4D book / by Lisa J. Amstutz.
Description: North Mankato, Minnesota : an imprint of Pebble, [2019] |
   Series: A+ books. A day in the life | Audience: Age 4–8.
Identifiers: LCCN 2018006117 (print) | LCCN 2018009143 (ebook) |
   ISBN 9781543515268 (eBook PDF) | ISBN 9781543515183 (hardcover) |
ISBN 9781543515220 (paperback)
Subjects: LCSH: Bald eagle—Life cycles—Juvenile literature.
Classification: LCC QL696.F32 (ebook) | LCC QL696.F32 A537 2019 (print) |
   DDC 598.9/43156—dc23
LC record available at https://lccn.loc.gov/2018006117

Editorial Credits
Gina Kammer, editor; Jennifer Bergstrom, designer;
Morgan Walters, media researcher; Laura Manthe, production specialist

Photo Credits
Dreamstime: Lynn Bystrom, 27; Getty Image: BirdImages, 18, Fuse, 21, Mark Newman, 17, 29, Paul Nicklen, 14, Tom Murphy, 25; Shutterstock: Birdiegal, 20, Brian E Kushner, 12, carlos.toledo, 24, CK_Images, 16, 22, Craig Mills, 13, critterbiz, 26, FloridaStock, Cover, Jean Faucett, 15, lana_elanor, Cover, design element throughout, Larry McCormick, 11, mary k Schmidt, 23, Mike Pellinni, 4, moosehenderson, 1, rck_953, 8, Rocksweeper, 9, Rocky Grimes, 5, schankz, 7, Silja R, 19, 30, Tsuguto Hayashi, 6

Note to Parents, Teachers, and Librarians

This book uses full color photographs and a nonfiction format to introduce the concept of a bald eagle's day. *A Day in the Life of a Bald Eagle* is designed to be read aloud to a pre-reader or to be read independently by an early reader. Photographs help listeners and early readers understand the text and concepts discussed. The book encourages further learning by including the following sections: Table of Contents, Glossary, Read More, Internet Sites, Critical Thinking Questions, and Index. Early readers may need assistance using these features.

Printed in the United States of America.
PA017

TABLE OF CONTENTS

A Bald Eagle's Day

As the sun comes up, a bald eagle wakes. She is hungry. It is time for breakfast!

The eagle stretches her wings. They measure 8 feet (2.4 meters) from tip to tip. That's longer than most beds! Her mate is smaller. His wingspan is only 6.6 feet (2 m).

About 7,000 feathers cover the eagle's body. They are brown and white. The feathers lift her into the air as she flaps her wings. She uses her tail feathers to turn and slow down.

FLAP!

The eagle's feathers keep her cool on hot days and warm on cold days. They keep her dry too.

The eagle lives near a lake where she can hunt. She flies to a high perch. She watches for food. She can see much better than you can. Look! A fish is swimming just below the water's surface.

LOOK!

WHOOSH! The eagle swoops. She snatches the fish with her feet. Fish are her main prey. But she is not a picky eater. She hunts crabs, turtles, mice, and smaller birds too. She will even eat dead animals and garbage!

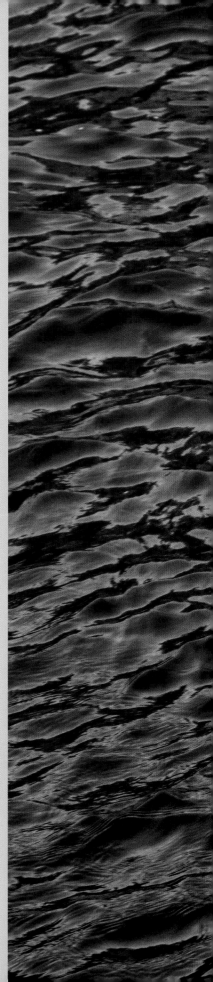

The eagle's talons dig into the fish and kill it.

These sharp claws are 2 inches (5.1 centimeters) long. Rough pads on the bird's feet help her grip the slippery fish.

The bald eagle carries the fish to her nest. The nest sits high in a tall tree. It measures 6 feet (1.8 m) wide and 4 feet (1.2 m) deep. The nest is made of sticks.

Soft grass, moss, and leaves line the nest.
The eagle and her mate add to it each year.

HOME!

CHEEP! CHEEP! Two chicks call for their mother. Soft down covers their bodies. It is fluffy and gray. Feathers will grow later.

CHEEP!

The chicks open their beaks wide. They are hungry. The eaglets need their parents to feed them. They will stay in the nest for about three months.

The eagle uses her sharp, curved beak to tear up the fish. She feeds it to the eaglets. They gulp down their meal. Now the eagle eats too. The food fills a pouch in her throat called a crop. Later it will move to her stomach. She will vomit out the bones.

SCREECH!

Uh-oh! Danger! A raccoon creeps
close to the tree with the nest.
The eagles must keep their chicks
safe. The male calls loudly.

SCREECH! He flies at the raccoon, showing his sharp beak and talons. The raccoon turns and runs away. The chicks are safe.

The eagle settles down with her chicks. Her mate flies off to hunt. The wind and his wings lift him 10,000 feet (3,000 m) into the air.

He soars at speeds up to 60 miles
(97 kilometers) per hour. He hunts for
a long time. But he does not find food.

SOAR!

An osprey flies by. It is holding a fish. The male eagle dives. He attacks the osprey until it drops the fish. Then the eagle swoops down to grab his prize. *SNATCH!* He carries the fish to the nest.

SNATCH!

After the family has eaten, the eagle preens her feathers. She cleans and smooths each feather with oil. The oil helps keep them dry.

As the sun sets, the eagle tucks her chicks under her wings. There they will stay warm and dry. She closes her eyes and waits for morning light.

Good night, bald eagle!

LIFE CYCLE OF A
BALD EAGLE

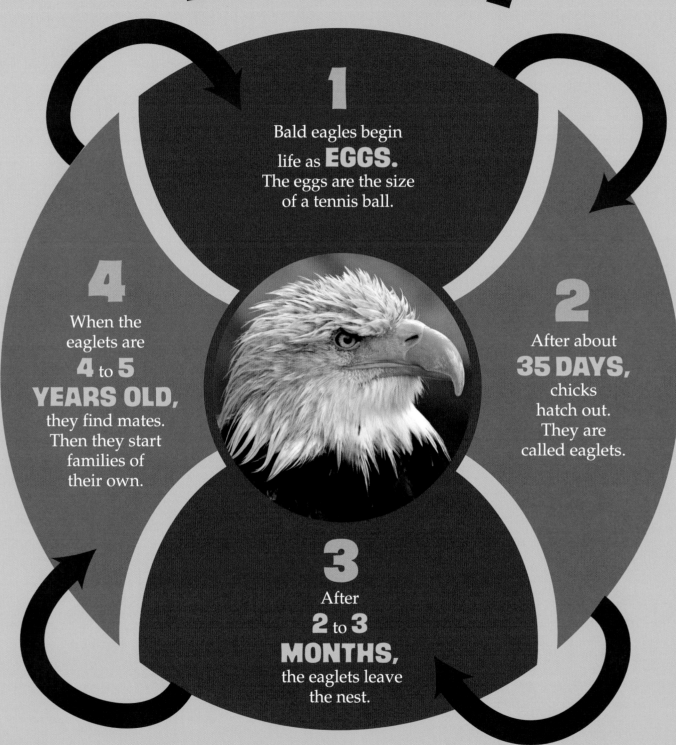

1
Bald eagles begin life as **EGGS.** The eggs are the size of a tennis ball.

2
After about **35 DAYS,** chicks hatch out. They are called eaglets.

3
After **2 to 3 MONTHS,** the eaglets leave the nest.

4
When the eaglets are **4 to 5 YEARS OLD,** they find mates. Then they start families of their own.

Glossary

crop—a pouch in a bird's throat where it can store food

down—the soft, fluffy feathers of a bird

mate—the male or female partner of a pair of animals

osprey—a large, brown hawk that eats mostly fish

perch—a place where a bird rests

preen—to clean and arrange feathers

prey—an animal hunted by another animal for food

talon—an eagle's claw; each foot has four toes, each with a very sharp, curved nail

vomit—to throw up food and liquid from the stomach out of the mouth

wingspan—the distance between the tips of a pair of wings when fully open

Read More

Bowman, Chris. *Bald Eagles*. North American Animals. Minneapolis: Bellwether Media, 2015.

Hansen, Grace. *Bald Eagles*. Animals of North America. Minneapolis: Abdo Kids, 2016.

Shea, Therese. *Saving the Endangered American Bald Eagle*. Conservation of Endangered Species. New York: Britannica Educational Publishing in Association with Rosen Educational Services, 2016.

Troupe, Thomas Kingsley. *I Want to Be a Bald Eagle*. I Want to Be . . . . North Mankato, Minn.: Picture Window Books, 2016.

Internet Sites

Use FactHound to find Internet sites related to this book.

Visit *www.facthound.com*

Just type in 9781543515183 and go.

Super-cool stuff! Check out projects, games and lots more at **www.capstonekids.com**

Critical Thinking Questions

1. Name three foods that are part of a bald eagle's diet.

2. Bald eagles use their talons to catch and kill prey. What are talons? Use the photos and glossary in this book to support your answer.

3. Name at least two ways that feathers help bald eagles.

4. Describe an eaglet, including how it looks, how it acts, and what it can and cannot do.

Index